LinkedIn Audit

Build a profile
that attracts opportunities

PUBLISHED BY: Diana Tanase

Diana Tanase

Table of Contents

Introduction

Welcome to *LinkedIn Audit: build a profile that attracts opportunities*!

In today's digital-first world, LinkedIn has become more than just a platform for job seekers. It's the heart of professional networking and personal branding. Your LinkedIn profile is your gateway to opportunities. It's where recruiters, potential employers, and collaborators come to evaluate who you are, what you've accomplished, and where you're heading.

This eBook is your comprehensive guide to turning your LinkedIn profile into a powerful tool that works for you. Whether you're aiming to land your dream job, attract clients, or establish yourself as a thought leader in your field, this guide will give you the strategies and confidence to stand out. It's not just about having a "good" profile; it's about having a profile that tells your story, reflects your expertise, and resonates with the people who matter.

LinkedIn Audit

Throughout this guide, we'll dive deep into the critical components of an optimized LinkedIn presence:

- How to craft a headline that makes people click.
- The secrets to writing an 'About' section that captivates and converts.
- Strategies for leveraging LinkedIn's hidden features, like analytics, keywords, and recommendations.
- Practical steps to grow your network, share meaningful content, and become discoverable by recruiters and clients alike.

But this isn't just a guide about technical optimization.
It's also about owning your professional narrative.
You'll learn how to highlight your unique strengths and present yourself authentically in a crowded digital landscape. Whether you're new to LinkedIn or looking to refine an already robust profile, this guide is your roadmap to success.

The journey to building an exceptional LinkedIn profile begins now. Let's make your LinkedIn presence as dynamic and impactful as you are.

1. Why your LinkedIn profile matters

LinkedIn is the world's largest professional network, and a powerful tool for job seekers, freelancers, and entrepreneurs.

Your LinkedIn profile serves as your digital business card, enabling recruiters, potential employers, and clients to find and evaluate you. In fact, 87% of recruiters use LinkedIn to vet candidates during the hiring process.

But LinkedIn is much more than a job board - it's a platform for building relationships, establishing your personal brand, and showcasing your skills.

Why LinkedIn is essential

1. Visibility

LinkedIn profiles are often the first result when someone Googles your name, giving you a chance to make a strong first impression.

2. Networking

LinkedIn allows you to connect with professionals, mentors, and peers, expanding your network and increasing your chances of landing opportunities.

3. Job searching

Many companies post exclusive job listings on LinkedIn, and the platform's job search feature allows you to apply for roles directly.

4. Building credibility

With recommendations, endorsements, and a strong portfolio, LinkedIn helps you build credibility within your industry.

To make the most of LinkedIn, it's important to create a complete, professional profile that showcases your skills, achievements, and personality.

2. Crafting a powerful headline

Your LinkedIn headline is one of the most important elements of your profile. It appears next to your name in search results, connection requests, and messages, making it a key factor in determining whether someone clicks on your profile.

What makes a great headline?

A great headline should be clear, concise, and reflective of both your skills and aspirations. Avoid the default setting (which usually shows your current job title) and instead, use the headline as an opportunity to explain what you do and the value you provide.

Examples:
- **Before:**
Marketing Manager at XYZ Company

- **After:**
Marketing Manager | Helping Companies Grow through Data-Driven Digital Campaigns

Key elements of a strong headline:

✓ **Clarity** ➡ make sure people understand what you do at a glance. Avoid vague terms like "Consultant" or "Specialist" without context.

✓ **Value proposition** ➡ focus on what you can offer. What problems do you solve, and how do you add value to your current or future employer?

✓ **Keywords** ➡ include relevant industry keywords that will help your profile appear in search results.

Actionable tips:

- Use vertical bars (|) to separate different roles or expertise areas.
- Avoid overused terms like "guru" or "expert" unless you have the credentials to back them up.
- Tailor your headline to the type of roles or connections you are trying to attract.

3. Writing a compelling 'About' section

The 'About' section is where you tell your professional story in your own words.

It's a chance to introduce yourself, explain your career journey, and highlight what you bring to the table.

What to include

1. **Introduction:** start with a brief introduction that captures your current role and career focus.

Example: "I'm a digital marketing strategist with over five years of experience in helping companies grow through data-driven campaigns."

2. **Career journey:** provide an overview of your career progression. What roles have you held, and what have you achieved in those roles? Highlight key accomplishments and skills.

3. **Unique value proposition:** explain what makes you different from others in your field. Focus on the

value you provide to your clients, employers, or team.

4. **Call-to-Action:** end with a call-to-action, inviting people to connect with you or learn more about your work.

Example: "Looking to collaborate on innovative marketing projects? Let's connect and explore how we can work together."

Writing style tips

- Write in the first person to make your profile feel more personal and approachable.
- Keep the tone professional, but don't be afraid to show your personality.
- Break up long paragraphs with bullet points or short sentences to improve readability.

4. Highlighting key skills with endorsements

The Skills section on LinkedIn allows you to showcase your top abilities and lets your network endorse you for them.

Endorsements provide social proof that you are skilled in specific areas, making your profile more credible.

Choosing the right skills:

1. **Relevance** ➡ focus on the skills that are most relevant to your industry and the type of work you want to attract.

2. **Specificity** ➡ instead of general skills like "Communication," choose more specific skills like "SEO Strategy," "Content Marketing," or "Project Management."

3. **Ranking** ➡ you can pin up to three skills at the top of your profile. Make sure your top skills align with the job or industry you're targeting.

How to get endorsements

- ***Endorse others.*** Start by endorsing others in your network. People are often willing to return the favour.

- ***Ask for endorsements***. You can ask close colleagues, former managers, or mentors to endorse your skills. Send a polite message explaining why their endorsement would be valuable.

- ***Skill rotation.*** Regularly update your top three skills to match the most relevant keywords for your current career goals.

5. Optimizing your work experience for LinkedIn

Just like a resume, your LinkedIn work experience section should showcase your accomplishments and demonstrate how you've added value to your previous employers. However, LinkedIn allows you more space to elaborate, so take advantage of the extra room to tell a fuller story.

How to optimize work experience

➢ *Use bullet points*
Break up long paragraphs into bullet points to make your experience more scannable.

➢ *Highlight achievements*
Focus on quantifiable results rather than just listing tasks.
Example: "Increased website traffic by 30% through targeted social media campaigns."

➢ *Include keywords*
Incorporate industry-relevant keywords from the job descriptions you're targeting.

➤ *Add media*

LinkedIn allows you to add images, presentations, or links to your work. If you have a portfolio, links to articles you've written, or project examples, include them here.

6. The importance of professional photos

Your LinkedIn profile picture is one of the first things people will notice. A professional, high-quality photo can create a strong first impression and increase your chances of being viewed or contacted.

Tips for a professional profile photo

1. Headshot ➡ make sure the photo is a clear, close-up shot of your face. Avoid full-body photos or anything too casual.
2. Dress appropriately ➡ wear attire that you would typically wear in a professional setting in your industry.
3. Background ➡ keep the background simple and uncluttered, so the focus remains on you.
4. Smile and eye contact ➡ a warm smile and direct eye contact can make your profile more approachable and inviting.

7. Creating and sharing engaging content

LinkedIn is not just a place to display your resume - it's also a platform for engaging with your professional network by sharing content.

Regularly posting articles, sharing industry news, and commenting on others' posts can increase your visibility and establish you as a thought leader.

Types of content to share

1. **Original articles.** Write posts or articles on topics relevant to your industry. This could be advice, case studies, or insights into market trends.

2. **Industry news**. Share and comment on news relevant to your field. Adding your own thoughts or insights can help spark conversations and showcase your expertise.

3. **Project highlights.** Share milestones or updates on projects you're working on. This demonstrates your active involvement in your field and keeps your network updated on your latest achievements.

Frequency of posts

Aim to post at least once a week to keep your profile active and stay top-of-mind with your network.

8. Leveraging LinkedIn recommendations

Recommendations on LinkedIn are powerful endorsements from your network that validate your skills and work experience.

These personal testimonials can boost your credibility and help you stand out to recruiters and potential employers.

A well-written recommendation from a former colleague, manager, or client is a form of social proof that reinforces the claims you've made on your profile.

How to get quality recommendations

✓ ***Request from relevant people*** ➠ ask for recommendations from people who have worked closely with you and can speak to your skills and achievements. This could include former managers, team members, or clients.

✓ **Be specific in your request** ➠ when asking for a recommendation, give the person guidance on what you'd like them to highlight. For example, if you're applying for marketing roles, you could ask them to focus on your campaign management skills or project leadership.

✓ **Offer to write a draft** ➡ if the person is busy or unsure of what to say, offer to write a draft that they can edit. This increases the chances that you'll get a recommendation that highlights the exact skills you want to showcase.

✓ **Give recommendations first** ➡ be generous with giving recommendations to others. This increases the likelihood that they will return the favour.

Where to place recommendations

LinkedIn automatically displays your most recent recommendations at the top, but you can reorder them to feature the most relevant ones.

For example, if you're applying for leadership roles, feature recommendations that highlight your management abilities.

9. Building a strong professional network

LinkedIn is a social platform at its core, and building a robust network is essential for expanding your opportunities.

Whether you're looking for new career opportunities, potential clients, or mentorship, having a broad and engaged network can open doors.

How to grow your network

- *Connect with people you know*
Start by connecting with colleagues, former coworkers, classmates, and mentors. These are the people who already know you and can help you expand your reach.

- *Personalize connection requests*
When sending a connection request to someone you don't know well, always include a personalized note explaining why you want to connect. Reference something specific about their work or profile that caught your attention.

- *Follow industry leaders*

Connect with or follow thought leaders in your industry. Engaging with their content through likes and comments can help you build relationships with them over time.

- *Join LinkedIn groups*

Groups are a great way to meet new professionals who share your interests. Participate in discussions and share valuable insights to build rapport with group members.

Maintaining relationships:

It's not enough to simply connect with people; you also need to nurture those relationships.

Regularly engage with your connections by commenting on their posts, sharing helpful content, or simply sending a quick message to stay in touch.

10. How to use LinkedIn for Job Searching

LinkedIn is one of the most powerful tools for job seekers, offering exclusive job postings, networking opportunities, and tools for applying directly to roles.

But to get the most out of LinkedIn's job search capabilities, you need to know how to use the platform effectively.

Tips for Job Searching on LinkedIn

1. Turn on the 'Open to Work' setting

Let recruiters know you're looking for a new role by enabling the 'Open to Work' feature. You can choose to make this visible only to recruiters or to everyone on the platform.

2. Use job filters

LinkedIn's job search tool allows you to filter jobs by location, industry, experience level, and more. Make sure to set alerts for new job postings that match your criteria.

3. **Apply directly through LinkedIn**

Many companies allow you to apply for roles directly through LinkedIn. Make sure your profile is fully optimized before applying, as employers may review it in addition to your resume.

4. **Reach out to hiring managers**

If you find a job posting that interests you, don't just apply - research the hiring manager or someone on the team and send them a personalized connection request. Mention your interest in the role and why you'd be a good fit.

LinkedIn job search features to explore:

- **Easy Apply** ➡ this feature allows you to apply for jobs with a single click, making the process fast and efficient.

- **Saved Jobs** ➡ save interesting job postings so you can return to them later.

- **Job Search Alerts** ➡ set up alerts for job postings that match your skills, location, and industry, so you'll be notified as soon as they're posted.

11. Utilizing LinkedIn analytics to track engagement

LinkedIn provides insights into how your profile is performing, including who has viewed your profile and how your posts are engaging your network.

Tracking these metrics can help you improve your profile and content over time.

Key analytics to monitor

- *Profile views* ➡ keep track of how many people are viewing your profile and who they are. If you're getting profile views from recruiters or hiring managers, it's a good sign that your profile is attracting the right attention.

- *Search appearances* ➡ this metric shows how many times your profile has appeared in search results and which keywords were used. This is particularly useful for optimizing your profile for ATS and recruiters.

- *Post engagement* ⟼ when you share content, LinkedIn provides insights into how many views, likes, comments, and shares your posts receive. Use this data to understand which types of content resonate most with your network.

How to improve your analytics

1. Increase engagement ⟼ if you notice low engagement on your posts, experiment with different types of content (e.g., articles, videos, polls) to see what works best.

2. Optimize your profile for searches ⟼ based on the keywords that people are using to find your profile, update your headline, summary, and skills section to align with popular search terms.

3. Follow Up on profile views ⟼ if a recruiter or potential client views your profile, send them a personalized message to introduce yourself and explore potential opportunities.

12. SEO for LinkedIn: using keywords to get found

Search engine optimization (SEO) isn't just for websites. It's also crucial for LinkedIn. By incorporating the right keywords into your profile, you increase the likelihood that recruiters and potential clients will find you when searching for candidates with your skills.

How to identify the right keywords

✓ **Job Descriptions** ➡ look at job listings for roles you're interested in and identify the most common keywords related to skills, job titles, and certifications. These are the words you'll want to include in your profile.

✓ **Industry terms** ➡ use industry-specific terms and jargon that reflect your expertise. For example, if you work in digital marketing, include terms like "SEO," "content strategy," or "social media marketing."

✓ **Recruiter search terms** ➡ think about how recruiters might search for candidates in your field. Use words and phrases that align with their search criteria.

Where to use keywords

➤ *Headline:* include a mix of your job title and core skills.

➤ *About section:* weave relevant keywords throughout your summary without keyword stuffing. Make sure it reads naturally.

➤ *Skills section:* highlight key skills that match the roles you're targeting.

➤ *Work experience*: incorporate keywords into your job descriptions to ensure your experience aligns with the search terms recruiters are using.

By optimizing your profile with the right keywords, you'll increase your chances of being found by recruiters, hiring managers, and other professionals in your industry.

13. How to stand out in LinkedIn groups

LinkedIn groups are an excellent way to engage with like-minded professionals, gain industry insights, and expand your network. However, simply joining groups isn't enough - you need to be an active participant to truly stand out.

How to engage effectively in groups

✓ Join relevant groups. Look for groups related to your industry, role, or specific interests. Choose active groups where members are regularly posting and engaging.

✓ Contribute value. Don't just observe. Share your insights, comment on discussions, and ask thoughtful questions. The more you contribute, the more visibility you'll gain.

✓ Share your expertise. Offer your expertise in group discussions by answering questions or sharing case studies. This positions you as a thought leader and builds your credibility.

✓ Build relationships: use group interactions as a way to build relationships with industry leaders. After engaging with someone in a group, consider sending them a connection request.

Types of posts that stand out

➢ Share relevant articles and ask for the group's thoughts.
➢ Start a discussion by asking for advice on a specific challenge you're facing.
➢ Post industry news or trends and ask how others are responding to it.

14. The Dos and Don'ts of LinkedIn etiquette

LinkedIn is a professional platform, and maintaining the right etiquette is key to building and sustaining relationships. Missteps can harm your reputation, while following best practices can help you build a strong professional presence.

Dos

> **Personalize connection requests**

Always include a personalized message when reaching out to someone you don't know well. Mention why you want to connect and how you can add value to their network.

> **Be active, but thoughtful**

Post regularly, but ensure that what you're sharing adds value to your network. Avoid posting too frequently or sharing irrelevant content.

➤ Engage with others

Comment on others' posts, congratulate them on their achievements, and offer insights on their content. Engagement fosters connection.

➤ Be professional

Remember that LinkedIn is a professional network, so maintain a courteous and respectful tone in all interactions.

Don'ts

➤ Avoid sales pitches

Don't send direct sales messages or pitches immediately after connecting with someone. Build a relationship first.

➤ Don't ignore messages

If someone takes the time to send you a thoughtful message or question, try to respond in a timely manner, even if it's brief.

➤ Don't spam your network

Avoid tagging large numbers of people in posts or sharing irrelevant content with your entire network. Spamming can lead to unfollows or disconnects.

15. Final Checklist: Is your LinkedIn Profile optimized?

Before considering your LinkedIn profile fully optimized, go through this comprehensive checklist to make sure every part of your profile is complete, polished, and working effectively for you.

PROFILE PICTURE

1. Is your profile picture a high-quality, professional headshot? (avoid casual photos, selfies, or cropped images that look unprofessional)

2. Are you dressed appropriately for your industry? (wear business or business-casual attire, depending on your field)

3. Is the background clean and uncluttered? (a simple, non-distracting background keeps the focus on you)

4. Does your expression convey approachability and confidence? (a smile and direct eye contact can make your profile more inviting)

HEADLINE

1. Does your headline clearly describe your current role or profession? (avoid generic titles like "Consultant" or "Specialist" without context)

2. Have you included a brief explanation of the value you provide? (use this space to highlight how you help solve problems or deliver results)

3. Are you using keywords that recruiters or clients might search for in your industry? (ensure your headline includes industry-specific terms that reflect your expertise)

4. Have you used a clean and concise format with separators like pipes (|) to list multiple roles or skills? (example: "Project Manager | Delivering Data-Driven Solutions for the Healthcare Sector")

ABOUT SECTION

1. Does your About section start with a strong introduction that immediately grabs attention? (include your current position, industry, and years of experience upfront)

2. Have you told your career story, outlining your professional journey and key achievements? (use this space to explain how your career has evolved, highlighting major accomplishments)

3. Have you emphasized your unique strengths and what sets you apart from others in your field? (include specific details about the problems you solve or the value you add to companies or clients)

4. Is your About section written in the first person to make it more personal and engaging? (example: "I am a digital marketing expert with a passion for helping small businesses grow.")

5. Have you ended the section with a call-to-action? (e.g., "Let's connect if you're looking to discuss marketing

strategies" - encourage readers to engage with you by inviting them to reach out or connect)

EXPERIENCE SECTION

1. Are your job descriptions more than just lists of responsibilities? (focus on specific achievements and the impact you made in each role)

2. Have you included metrics wherever possible? (e.g., increased sales by 20%, managed a team of 10 - numbers make your achievements more concrete and impressive)

3. Are you incorporating industry-relevant keywords into each job description to optimize for LinkedIn search? (include terms from the job descriptions you're targeting)

4. Are you using bullet points to break up text and make your experience easy to scan? (avoid long paragraphs that are harder to read)

5. Are the dates for each job correct, and do they clearly show the duration of your employment? (include both the month and year for start and end dates)

EDUCATION SECTION

1. Have you accurately listed your degrees, certifications, and any relevant coursework? (include the name of the institution, the degree earned, and the year of completion)

2. Have you listed any certifications that are relevant to your industry? (include certifications like PMP, CPA, or Lean Six Sigma if applicable)

3. Have you omitted irrelevant education or old courses that don't add value to your profile? (only include education that is pertinent to your career)

SKILLS AND ENDORSEMENTS

1. Have you listed the most relevant skills for your current job or the roles you're targeting? (the top three skills should align with the keywords recruiters are likely to search for)

2. Do your top skills have multiple endorsements from colleagues or peers? (aim to get endorsements for the most important skills to increase credibility)

3. Is there a mix of hard (technical) skills and soft skills in your list? (example: Include both "SEO Strategy" (hard skill) and "Leadership" (soft skill)

4. Have you removed outdated or irrelevant skills that no longer reflect your expertise? (keep your skills list focused on your current industry and career goals)

RECOMMENDATIONS

1. Do you have at least two strong recommendations from colleagues, managers, or clients? (recommendations provide social proof of your skills and work ethic)

2. Are the recommendations specific, highlighting particular projects or achievements? (a strong recommendation focuses on concrete examples of your contributions)

3. Have you written recommendations for others in your network? (giving thoughtful recommendations increases the likelihood that people will reciprocate)

PROFILE MEDIA AND LINKS

1. Have you added media (e.g., presentations, articles, or portfolios) to showcase your work? (visual elements make your profile more engaging and help demonstrate your expertise)

2. Have you included links to personal websites, blogs, or portfolios that are relevant to your profession? (if you're in a creative or technical field, links to projects are essential)

NETWORKING AND ENGAGEMENT

1. Are you actively growing your network by connecting with people in your industry or desired field? (aim to connect with people who can help advance your career or provide insights)

2. Are you sending personalized notes when connecting with people you don't know well? (a brief message explaining why you want to connect increases the chances of acceptance)

3. Are you regularly liking, commenting on, or sharing posts from your network? (engaging with content helps you stay visible and build relationships with your connections)

CONTENT AND POSTS

1. Are you sharing valuable content on LinkedIn at least once a week? (consistent posting keeps you active and increases your visibility in your network)

2. Are you sharing a mix of articles, personal insights, industry news, and professional updates? (a variety of content keeps your audience engaged and showcases your expertise)

3. Have you written any articles or posts that demonstrate your knowledge and insights into industry trends? (this establishes you as a thought leader and builds your credibility)

JOB SEARCH FEATURES

1. Have you enabled the "Open to Work" feature if you're looking for new opportunities? (this signals to recruiters that you're actively searching for a role)

2. Have you set up job alerts for positions that match your skills and experience? (receiving alerts helps you stay on top of new job postings)

3. Are you following companies you're interested in working for to stay updated on their job postings and company news? (this keeps you informed about potential openings and developments in your target companies)

LINKEDIN URL
FINAL REVIEW AND POLISH

1. Have you customized your LinkedIn profile URL for a more professional and memorable link? (example: "linkedin.com/in/YourName" instead of a string of numbers)

2. Have you checked your profile for spelling and grammatical errors using tools like Grammarly? (typos can make your profile look unprofessional)

3. Is your formatting (e.g., font size, bullet points, section headings) consistent throughout your profile? (consistency in style makes your profile easier to read and more professional)

4. Is the information on your LinkedIn profile consistent with your resume? (ensure there are no discrepancies between your LinkedIn profile and your resume)

5. Have you viewed your profile on both desktop and mobile devices to ensure it looks good across all platforms? (many recruiters and connections will view your profile on mobile devices)

This expanded checklist ensures that your LinkedIn profile is fully optimized from top to bottom. By following this detailed guide, you can make sure that your profile attracts the right opportunities, builds your personal brand, and showcases your expertise in the best possible light.

16. Final steps to optimize your LinkedIn profile for maximum impact

Before wrapping up your LinkedIn profile optimization journey, there are a few additional steps you can take to ensure your profile is working as hard as it can for you. These final touches will help you maximize the potential of your profile for networking, job searching, and professional growth.

PERSONAL URL CUSTOMIZATION

LinkedIn allows you to create a custom URL for your profile, which makes it easier to share and more professional-looking. Instead of a URL with random numbers, you can have something like "linkedin.com/in/YourName".

How to customize your URL

✓ Go to your profile and click on "Edit public profile & URL" in the top right corner.

✓ In the new window, click the pencil icon next to your URL and customize it with your full name or professional title.

Why it matters

A custom URL is more memorable and professional. It also looks cleaner on your resume, business card, or email signature.

SHOWCASE SERVICES
(for Freelancers and Consultants)

LinkedIn allows you to highlight specific services you offer on your profile. This is especially useful for freelancers, consultants, and small business owners who want to attract clients.

How to add services to your profile

✓ Navigate to your LinkedIn profile and click the "Open to" button below your profile photo.

✓ Select "Providing Services" and fill out the details of the services you offer, such as content writing, digital marketing, business consulting, etc.

Benefits of showcasing services

➢ It makes it easier for potential clients to understand what you offer and contact you directly.

➢ This section increases your visibility in searches when people are looking for professionals in your field.

UTILIZING LINKEDIN FEATURES LIKE 'CREATOR MODE' (for Thought Leaders)

LinkedIn introduced Creator Mode, a feature that's designed for professionals who want to build their brand by sharing content and growing their following.

How to enable creator mode

1. Click "View Profile."
2. Scroll to the "Resources" section and click on "Creator Mode."

3. Follow the prompts to turn it on and choose the topics you want to be known for.

Why use Creator Mode?

- Increased visibility ➡ with Creator Mode, LinkedIn highlights your posts more prominently, helping you gain followers.

- Profile layout change ➡ your profile will display your content more prominently, and instead of a "Connect" button, it will show a "Follow" button, encouraging people to follow your updates.

REGULARLY UPDATE YOUR PROFILE

Your LinkedIn profile isn't a "set it and forget it" type of tool. It should evolve as your career grows.

Regularly updating your profile ensures it reflects your current skills, projects, and achievements, which keeps you relevant to recruiters and connections.

LinkedIn Audit

Things to update regularly

➤ New skills: if you complete a new course, learn a new skill, or earn a certification, make sure to add it to your profile immediately.

➤ Work experience: update your job descriptions when you take on new responsibilities, complete a project, or get promoted.

➤ Engagement: continue posting content, engaging with your network, and joining relevant conversations to maintain an active presence.

Diana Tanase

SUGGESTED LINKEDIN PROFILE OPTIMIZATION PROCESS (for Step-by-Step Improvement)

Here's a breakdown of how you can structure the process of optimizing your LinkedIn profile over time, using this eBook as a guide:

Week 1: Basic Profile Setup

✓ Update headline: craft a compelling headline that reflects your expertise and includes relevant keywords.

✓ Add a professional photo: ensure you have a clear, professional headshot as your profile picture.

✓ Write the About section: focus on your career story and unique value proposition. Make it engaging and in the first person.

Week 2: Work Experience and Skills

✓ Update work experience: add detailed descriptions for your current and past jobs, focusing on achievements and quantifiable results.

✓ Add media and projects: showcase your work by linking to relevant articles, presentations, or projects.

✓ Optimize skills: add relevant skills to your profile and ensure your top three skills are highlighted for endorsements.

Week 3: Building Credibility

✓ Request recommendations: reach out to former colleagues or managers for recommendations that highlight your strengths.

✓ Engage with content: start sharing or commenting on posts that are relevant to your industry. This boosts your visibility and builds your credibility as an active member of your professional community.

✓ Join LinkedIn groups: start participating in discussions and contributing your insights.

Week 4: Networking and Job Searching

✓ Expand your network: connect with people in your industry, thought leaders, and recruiters to build relationships.

✓ Activate 'Open to Work' or 'Providing Services' options: let recruiters know you're open to new opportunities or showcase the services you offer if you're a freelancer or consultant.

✓ Engage in Job Search: set job alerts, apply for relevant jobs, and reach out to hiring managers or connections in your target companies.

ONGOING: MAINTENANCE

- **Monitor analytics**

➠ use LinkedIn's analytics tools to track your profile views, search appearances, and post engagement. Adjust your profile as needed to improve your visibility.

- **Continue posting content**

➠ share articles, insights, and updates to keep your profile active and relevant.

- **Refine your keywords**

➠ periodically review job descriptions in your field and update your profile with the latest industry keywords to stay relevant.

Diana Tanase

Conclusion

Congratulations on reaching the end of *LinkedIn Audit: build a profile that attracts opportunities*! You've taken the first - and perhaps most important - step toward transforming your LinkedIn presence into a tool that opens doors to opportunities.

Thank you for choosing this guide to support you along the way. I can't wait to see how your LinkedIn presence transforms and the opportunities it unlocks for you.

You now have all the tools you need to optimize your LinkedIn profile and start attracting new opportunities. Whether you're a job seeker, freelancer, entrepreneur, or seasoned professional, a well-optimized LinkedIn profile can be a game-changer in growing your network, showcasing your expertise, and landing new opportunities.

Are you ready to take your LinkedIn presence to the next level?

Start implementing these strategies today, and watch your profile transform into a powerful tool for personal branding, job searching, and professional growth.

A well-optimized LinkedIn profile is not just a static page; it's a living representation of your professional journey. It evolves with your career, adapts to new goals, and reflects the value you bring to the table. With the strategies and insights from this book, you now have everything you need to:

- Showcase your expertise with confidence.
- Build meaningful connections that align with your aspirations.
- Attract recruiters, clients, and collaborators who see your potential.

Remember, LinkedIn is more than a professional network; it's a space to build your personal brand, tell your story, and create new possibilities. Whether you're using it to explore career opportunities, establish yourself as a leader in your field, or simply connect with like-minded professionals, your LinkedIn profile is your virtual handshake to the world.

Take the time to revisit and refine your profile regularly. Stay consistent in sharing content, engaging with your network, and updating your accomplishments. The effort you invest will not only enhance your visibility but also amplify your credibility in your chosen field.

Your professional growth is in your hands - own it, share it, and let your LinkedIn profile reflect the remarkable journey you're on.

If you're looking for personalized help with your LinkedIn strategy or profile optimization, let's connect! I'd love to help you achieve your professional goals.